JUSTIN FLETCHER

Illustrated by Patrick Tate

What clothes do you wear when it rains?

Thunderpants.

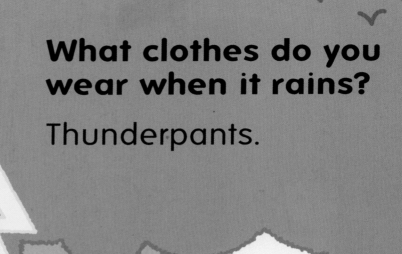

What did one raindrop say to the other raindrop?

My plop is bigger than your plop.

What's the hottest day of the week?

Sunday.

Knock, knock.
Who's there?
Dunnup.
Dunnup who?
Yuck.

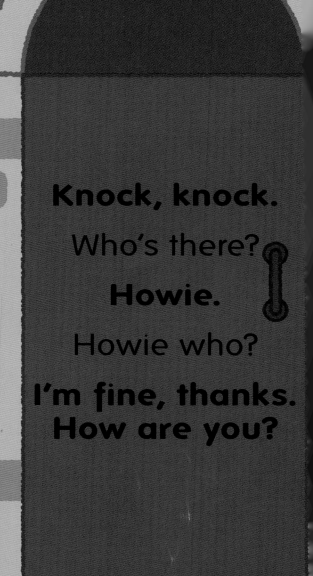

Knock, knock.
Who's there?
Howie.
Howie who?
**I'm fine, thanks.
How are you?**

Knock, knock.

Who's there?

Justin.

Justin who?

Justin time for tea.

Why did the dog have a banana in its ear?

It wasn't eating properly.

What's brown and sticky?

A stick.

What type of dog do you find in a toilet?

A poo-dle.

Who is really, really big and wears glass slippers?

Cinder-elephant.

What do gorillas sing at Christmas?

'Jungle bells!'

Why do giraffes have long necks?

Because their feet smell.

What is a rabbit's favourite treat?

Lolli-hops.

How does a
chicken tell
the time?

One o'cluck,
two o'cluck . . .

it's four o'cluck!

What did the sea say to the sand?

Nothing, it just waved.

What are the strongest creatures in the sea?

Mussels.

Why was the beach wet?

Because the seaweed.

What do you call an angry pea?

Grump-pea.

What is orange and sounds like a parrot?

A carrot.

Why did the toilet paper roll down the hill?

To get to the bottom.

What music are balloons scared of?

Pop music.

What makes music on your hair?

A head band.

Why did the cow push the farmer?

Because he wanted him to mooove.

What was the bull doing in the field with his eyes closed?

Bull-dozing.

Knock, knock.

Who's there?

Interrupting cow.

Interrupting C—

MOO!

Why do witches wear name badges?

So they can tell which witch is which.

Aa Bb Cc Dd Ee Ff Gg

Hh Ii Jj Kk Ll Mm Nn

Oo Pp Qq Rr Ss Tt Uu

Vv Ww Xx Yy Zz

What do elves learn in school?

The elf-abet.

What instrument do skeletons like to play?

The trom-bone.

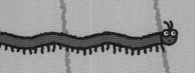

What goes 'Ho, ho, ho, plonk'?

Santa laughing his head off.

What did one snowman say to the other?

Do you smell carrots?

What do snowmen eat for breakfast?

Snowflakes.

What do you call a one-eyed dinosaur?

Do-you-think-he-saw-us.

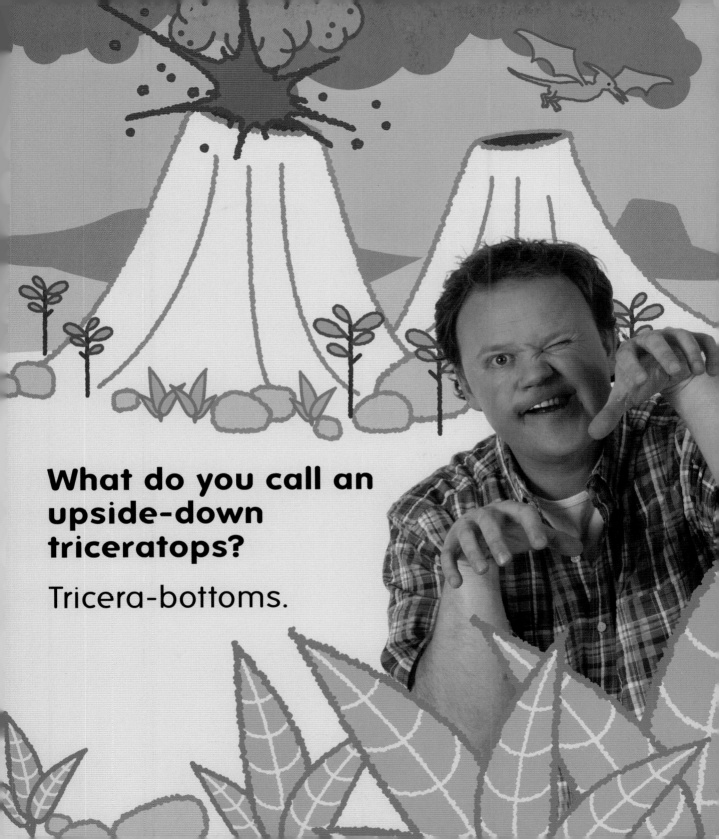

What do you call an upside-down triceratops?

Tricera-bottoms.

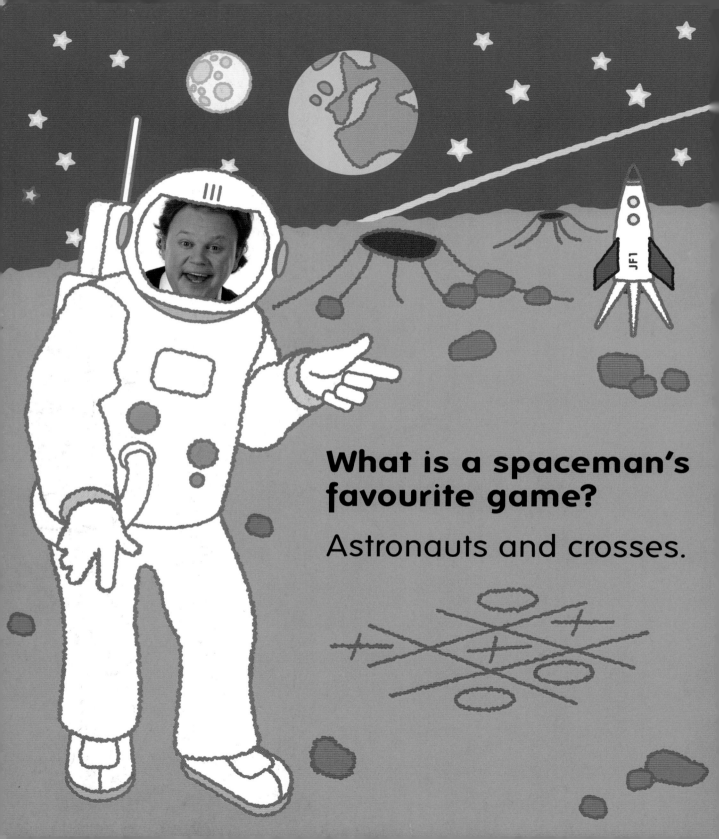

What is a spaceman's favourite game?

Astronauts and crosses.

Why did the spaceship land outside the bedroom?

The landing light was on.

What are an alien's favourite sweeties?

Martian-mallows.

Where do baby apes go to sleep?

Ape-ri-cots.

What are pets' favourite bedtime stories?

Furry tales.

Knock, knock.

Who's there?

Bed.

Bed who?

Better go to sleep.

More giggle-tastic jokes from Justin!

First published in Great Britain in 2012
by Faber and Faber Ltd
Bloomsbury House
74–77 Great Russell Street
London WC1B 3DA
Designed by Patrick Tate
Printed and bound in China
All rights reserved

© Justin Fletcher, 2012

Illustrations © Patrick Tate, 2012

A CIP record for this book is available from the British Library

ISBN 978–0–571–28823–6
2 4 6 8 10 9 7 5 3 1